The High Cost of Resentment

The Journey to Freedom

———⊗⊗⊗———

by

Arni Jacobson

with
Bob Mims

XULON
PRESS

Resentment is when the expiration date on forgiveness passes without resolve. It sours our lives and those we love. Without a doubt, resentment is the social cancer that is decaying and destroying our world. Many of the very leaders that should be bringing solutions are in fact victims themselves. My longtime friend Arni Jacobson has taken his personal pain, and with deep passion, methodically diagnoses and treats the virus that is often veiled in denial. The vulnerability of his story is shocking. The journey of his found freedom–nothing short of sensational. Please read this book!

–Pastor Phil Munsey

Chairman of Champion Network of Pastors

Joel Osteen/Lakewood Church, Houston, TX

Resentment carries a high price tag. In this book by my friend and fellow board member of Church Growth International, Arni Jacobson shares the deep anguish of soul he endured and triumphed over in a trial of resentment. Why not let this book be the moment your life gets set free from past hurts, wounds, and disappointments? Like Joseph, the revelation of victory over resentment will open new doors of opportunity for you!

–Pastor Larry Stockstill

Pastor, Missionary, and Worldwide Evangelist

Author of Best-Selling Book, *The Remnant*

Pastor Arni Jacobson is a great Pastor, friend, and ministry associate. I have personally walked through the situations with him that he details in this book, and I have also watched him overcome his feelings of resentment that had a strong hold on his life. You will definitely want to read this book.

–Pastor Steve Riggle

President of Grace International in Houston, TX

Founder and Senior Pastor of

Grace Community Church in Houston, TX

President of King's University in Van Nuys, CA

Pastor Arni Jacobson has been a father-figure for as long as I can remember. I served on his staff for 10 years, and he helped form me into the Pastor that I have become. He is a successful soul-winner, a mega-church planter and builder, an incredible Pastor, and an inspired author. Anyone who has struggled or is struggling with resentment will want to read this book – it is a winner.

–Pastor Dale Oquist

Lead Pastor of The People's Church, Fresno, CA

My good friend Pastor Arni Jacobson has written a great book from his personal experience of resentment. It is a must-read.

–Pastor Rich Wilkerson

Evangelist, Author, and Pastor

Trinity Church, Miami, FL

Chances are, at some point in your life you have either hurt or been hurt by someone. Sadly, this often leads to a path of broken hearts and broken relationships with the aftermath of people carrying the terrible burden of bitterness and resentment. In these pages, Arni Jacobson shows how the path towards bitterness is a lot easier than the path away from it, but brilliantly shows us the way to healing. God calls us to do what is sometimes difficult to do: forgive. Thankfully, what He calls us to do, He enables us to do. Sometimes we are injured and sometimes we are the instruments of injury. Rather than getting trapped in a cycle of offense and defense, there is great freedom when we come to the cross and just decide to let go and let God.

–Pastor Mark Gungor

Founder of *Laugh Your Way to a Better Marriage* Ministry

Senior Pastor of Celebration Church, Green Bay, WI

Dear Reader,

There is a tremendous cost to those who carry resentment. The good news is you don't have to hold on to it forever. In this book, I will share my personal journey of resentment and how it had control over my life some time before I made the decision to give it completely to God.

I had an interesting experience as I was watching a movie on TV not long ago. It was about a man's wife who had been killed in a car accident, and the man blamed a woman who he thought was responsible for her death. He searched and searched, and after twenty years, located the woman with the intent to kill her (the police foiled that plan). The woman wanted to talk to the man in custody, but before she was brought in to express her regrets, the detective said these unforgettable words to the man: "RESENTMENT WILL DESTROY ANY CONTAINER IT IS CARRIED IN." My heart leaped as I thought about how true this statement was.

Following each chapter, you will have the opportunity to **reflect** (discuss what you took away from the chapter),

relate (consider how it relates to your personal life), and **respond** (ask God to help you in these areas). This is a great way to dig deeper into the book and into your own life as you move forward past resentment.

At the end of the book you will find a "30 Days to Freedom Challenge" for overcoming resentment in your life. After you journal for the day, you will find a section called "Praise / Prayer." This is a great place for you to write down praises to God for what He has done and prayer requests. After you write these down, I encourage you to pray to God. Thank Him for His faithfulness, and present your prayer requests to Him. Prayer works! There are also three verses during your challenge for you to memorize. These verses will be essential for you as you work through any hurt, betrayal, or unforgiveness in your life.

My prayer for you as you read this little book is that you will empty your container of resentment and bitterness, before it destroys you. I hope the message will infiltrate your heart and change you by setting you free from any resentment you are holding on to.

God Bless,
Rev. Arni Jacobson

DEDICATION

------∞∞∞------

I dedicate this book to those who will find victory over RESENTMENT. They can then pray the words from the hymn Martin Luther King quoted in his unforgettable speech: *"Free at last! Free at last! Thank God Almighty, I am free at last!"*

Introduction

Resentment.

The Merriam-Webster Dictionary defines it in various ways: "A lingering ill will towards a person for a real or imagined wrong." Alternatively, the word might embody "a painful awareness of another's possessions or advantages and a desire to have them too." Finally, *resentment* can be "the feeling of being offended or resentful after a slight or indignity."

If you live long enough, you *will* experience resentment:

— The premature death of a loved one can bring resentment towards God, other family members, or even guilt that turns resentment inward.

— A child discovers it when seeing a parent favor a sibling, or when he or she is chosen last (or left out entirely) on the playground when teams are picked.

— A teenager feels it when he or she is rejected by the "in crowd," or when that first love ends in a breakup.

— As an adult, resentment smolders when a promotion at work goes to another or layoffs bring unemployment.

— A marriage disintegrates due to unfaithfulness.

— A business partnership falls apart.

— A treasured friendship turns to bitterness over a wrong done or perceived.

— Resentment often is planted in the bruised human soul by physical, emotional or sexual abuse by a family member, or even a church leader.

Yes, if you are human, you know resentment, and none of Webster's definitions convey the depth, pain and crippling bitterness, depression and anger you can feel when you find yourself drowning in the dark pit that is *Resentment* — with a capital R.

I know because I have been there.

Without the grace of our Lord Jesus Christ, I likely would still be there, being consumed from the inside out by the memories of offenses, the betrayals I felt, the painful emotional blows received, and the occasional fantasies of retaliation that fought for a foothold in my mind during the darkest nights of my soul. You would be right to be sobered hearing this admission by anyone claiming to be a Christian. To hear it from a minister of the gospel–a messenger of God's love, forgiveness, salvation and peace–might be even more of an unpleasant surprise.

I will go further. You would be right to be shocked, if you had known me during any time of my more than three decades of pastoring, that Arni Jacobson would confess to having been plagued by the veritable Mother of all Resentment. After all, my public persona has consistently been that of an upbeat, optimistic guy who never turns off his zeal for sharing the plan of salvation – whether from behind a pulpit or talking to a fellow passenger on a jet liner or a waiter or waitress at a restaurant.

Nonetheless, that was me, and not so long ago.

In preaching this message about *Resentment* in churches throughout the United States and in congregations overseas, I learned that I have not been alone. When I ask people to come forward for prayer – to seek God's power to let their resentment go, to forgive and be forgiven – repeatedly the response has been nearly unanimous.

I have heard hundreds of stories about how resentment took root in the lives of Christians, and how – like me – the roots grew deep and increasingly bitter. People once filled with joy and love for their brothers and sisters, effective workers and leaders in their churches and examples of the life-changing power of Christ at work, at school and in their own homes, losing their way.

Resentment is indeed part of the general human condition, a truth underscored for me unexpectedly not long ago when I was interviewed for a television special on the late Ray Nitschke, the legendary linebacker for the Green Bay Packers football team.

Ray and his wife, Jackie, had come to Christ through my ministry. When Ray died of a heart attack in 1998, I had the honor of preaching his funeral in Green Bay, a goodbye that packed our church and was also aired on live television.

After the filming wrapped up, I got to talking with the interviewer and crew. They asked me what I was doing, and I told them about this book. The discussion turned to forgiveness and resentment and how one can free you, while the other imprisons you body, mind and spirit.

It was like a bright light went on for these folks. One person admitted to being bitter over being cheated out of $50,000 in a business deal. Another said past abuse had left her deep in resentment. A cameraman asked me to make sure he got a copy of the book – which I gladly promised.

When unresolved, resentment can cripple or even kill you spiritually – and today's news headlines are full of cases where those consequences actually end in permanent physical injury, or in a cemetery.

Everywhere I have shared this message, in churches, on a plane or as a TV crew packed up its gear, I have heard about the high cost of resentment. In this book, I will share my own story with you, and that of a boy in the Bible named Joseph, whose own struggle with resentment lays out God's path to freedom, forgiveness and reconciliation.

Read the following seven short chapters of this message, which birthed a radical change in my life. My prayer is that you too will be set free.

Chapter One

The Pain of Empty Promises and Betrayal

*E*veryone can tell you stories about "empty promises."
Maybe it involves something as simple as being stood
up for a date or being denied an expected promotion or raise.
It might be something more heartbreaking, such as betrayed
marriage vows that leave a lifetime of trust shattered.

Whatever the case, these were promises that proved no
more valuable than $1 million check drawn on a drained
bank account.

There is happiness in seeing a trusted friend's integrity
proved true with a promise made and delivered; it is reas-
suring, a testament of faith, and you overflow with gratitude.
Instead of appreciation, empty promises may overwhelm the

betrayed with disappointment, hurt, and anger, and plant the seeds of long-term resentment.

There is a high cost to pay for such resentment, and the longer it churns inside your heart, the toll compounds like interest on a loan shark's dollar. Resentment blossoms with thorns of bitterness, choking out your joy in Christ and suffocating your ability to share God's love with others.

Resentment even brings depression that can affect your health, starve your friendships, stress family relationships and drag down your performance on the job.

More than 20 years ago, my wife Jan and I moved our family to Green Bay, Wisconsin to start a church. We believed in God's promises so much that we threw our savings into underwriting the endeavor. God was faithful; the church grew from a handful of folks meeting in a borrowed school into a large congregation of thousands worshiping on its own multi-million-dollar campus. Thousands of people first met and accepted Christ under our ministry there.

In 2005, as we moved into our sixties, Jan and I looked forward to a semi-retirement. Our church had long before set up a retirement plan that would pay us a portion of our former salary for the rest of our lives. When our son, Chad, felt called to start a new church in Salt Lake City, the church also committed to pay his and an associate pastor's salaries for the first year to help pioneer the new work.

A few months after we had all moved to Utah, those promises turned out to be empty. The new pastor notified me that due to financial challenges, not only was my retirement pay suspended, perhaps permanently, but the church also would have to break its promise to support the new Salt Lake City church's pastors during their crucial first year.

Empty promises...broken promises. They hit me and my family like a fast-moving car in a crosswalk . . . followed by a pickup truck, a semi-trailer tractor rig and then a two-mile-long freight train. At an age where we expected to be slowing down a bit, my wife Jan and I found ourselves without our expected income, and were forced to use whatever savings we had to keep the new church's pioneering effort alive.

The resentment born of hurt, shock and disbelief at this betrayed trust and abandonment, took root. I was in an emotional pit, mired in the mud of helpless rage. Without realizing it, all that anger, bitterness and inner turmoil began to forge spiritual chains on me. I was becoming a slave to resentment.

It took me two years to allow the Holy Spirit to finally heal my wounded soul and open my eyes to see the path out of the pit and to a place where God could break off the chains of resentment.

It is not the first time God had to take one of His children by the hand, turning tragedy into hope and betrayal into blessing. His name? Joseph. His story begins in Genesis 37:1. At age 17, Joseph had it made. He was his father, Jacob's, favorite son, the offspring of his true love, Rachel. The boy had become even more precious to the old man when Rachel died in giving birth to Joseph's only other full-blooded brother, Benjamin.

As a sign of his favor, Jacob had covered Joseph in the famous "coat of many colors," the Armani suit of Old Testament times. That gift of love to Joseph didn't endear the boy to his eleven half-brothers, and the boys were jealous seeing that coat and its wearer coming through the fields for their dad, who had made it a habit to have Joseph spy on their work – or lack of it – tending the flocks.

The brothers did not like Joseph, and that was not all their fault. Lots of preachers, recounting the story, make the brothers into devils incarnate. No doubt what they ended up doing to their own kin was devious – but considering the roots of their resentment, you might cut them a little slack.

Their father, Jacob, had talked his own starving brother, Esau, into trading his birthright for a pot of stew. Then when their dad was dying, Jacob tricked the blind old man into giving him the blessing due to Esau as first-born. What goes around comes around. Later, it was Jacob who was cheated. After working seven years for the right to marry Rebekah, Jacob's father-in-law instead slipped his older daughter, a less attractive Leah, into the darkened wedding tent. Jacob had to work another seven years to get Rebekah.

Talk about resentment! Jacob knew all about it, and not just from that wedding night switcheroo. Father-in-law Laban also cheated his son-in-law in a number of business deals before Jacob finally broke loose.

The two sons he had with his true love, Rebekah – Joseph and Benjamin – were his favorites. What about Leah's children? One can imagine that while Jacob certainly loved his sons, he could not look at them without occasional reminders of that wedding night betrayal.

Leah's sons almost certainly knew this. Joseph did not help himself any by giving Jacob a bad report from time to time – and then there were those dreams the kid shared.

One was about the family out harvesting wheat and Joseph's sheaf suddenly standing upright, and the brothers' sheaves bowing down to it. Another dream had stars representing the brothers – and even the sun and moon, symbolizing Jacob and stepmother Leah, bowing in submission before Joseph's star.

So, one day Joseph was dispatched again to check up on the crew. The brothers saw him coming – that coat must have been a dazzler – and started plotting.

"Look, this dreamer is coming. Come therefore, let us now kill him and cast him into some pit; and we shall say, 'Some wild beast has devoured him.' We shall see what becomes of his dreams!" (Genesis 37:19-20 NKJV)

The eldest brother, Reuben, was no fan of Joseph either; but he also was no killer. So he talked his siblings into just tossing their brother into an empty cistern, with the idea of sneaking back later to free the boy.

It did not work out that way, though. While Reuben was away – checking on the goats and sheep perhaps – the boys spotted some Ishmaelite traders coming along in a camel caravan. Judah came up with the idea of making some coin on the kid, if they could not kill him.

Sell Joseph to the Ishmaelites! Genius idea, the brothers agreed. No fraternal blood spilled; a bag full of silver coins; and Joseph out of the picture, for good! Win-win. So, they hauled their brother up and turned him over to the chains of the traders for twenty shekels of silver – about $100 in today's currency.

Really, that was not much of a price for a perfectly good teenage slave. But then, they did keep that nice coat; they needed it to soak with goat's blood for when they told a distraught Jacob that his cherished son had been dinner for an especially nasty predator. Probably a lion or a cave bear, hyenas . . . any would do for the lie.

Reuben came back ready to rescue Joseph . . . only to find him gone. He was the eldest and had failed. He felt badly, no doubt. However, he did not feel bad enough to take responsibility, so he went along with the plot to deceive dear old Dad.

The old man took it hard. He bought the brothers' tale, convinced his favorite son was torn to pieces and eaten by an animal. All that was left was the torn and bloodied coat put into his hands, and days of weeping ahead.

I think there was more than a few tears and sobs from Joseph too as he trudged through the sands of the Sinai Desert toward Egypt and the slave markets. The shackles probably chafed his wrists raw, the sun burning his shoulders. At some point on that journey, each step further away from the love and favor he had known his whole life, I will bet those tears transformed from grief to hot rivulets of anger.

Bitterness and resentment must have hovered around Joseph like ghosts, whispering about betrayal, seething with fear and anger, and even the beginning thoughts of revenge.

It is what Joseph did with those feelings of fear, abandonment and hopelessness that made all the difference.

He turned to the only remaining constant, the sole foundation in life left to him: *his faith in God.*

Reflect: What are some thoughts from this chapter?

_____

_____

_____

_____

_____

_____

_____

_____

Relate: How does this relate to your personal life and experiences?

_____

_____

_____

_____

_____

_____

_____

_____

Respond: Write a prayer to God asking for direction and help in these areas.

_____

_____

_____

_____

_____

_____

_____

_____

_____

_____

Chapter Two

Riptide of Resentment

*T*he high cost of resentment is not paid all at once. It is not a case of being hammered, reeling around dizzy for a few moments, and then taking a deep breath or two and moving on.

Ever been caught under the breakers on an ocean beach? A big wave crests and crashes down on you, sending you face-first into the sand. The tide recedes and you think, "Wow. That felt like a wet mountain, but it's gone. I think I'll get up and go back to building sand castles."

Then another wave flattens you. And another. Finally, you crawl out of the surf, sputtering water out of your lungs, tears mixing with the salt water and kelp on your face, and lie on the sand gasping for air. In a few moments of panic, you feel like you have lived an eternity of terror.

That is how resentment begins. That is how it feels. The emotions simmer, the pain and shock of betrayal gradually transforming from burning hurt to a cold and growing rage.

That is how it was for me in Utah, where just a few months into our move the impact of our loss of financial support became a numbing reality. Each new bill received and check written on our dwindling savings to keep the new Salt Lake City ministry and us afloat was a bitter reminder of promises made and broken.

Resentment feeds on itself. The memories of betrayal soon give way to fantasies about revenge. Your mind writes screenplays of retribution, and your imagination flips on the internal projector to display movies of malevolence.

You may hope for disaster to strike on your nemesis; for him or her to feel the same pain that was inflicted on you. For an instant, such thoughts might give you a bit of a rush – before a wave of shame send you to your knees, seeking forgiveness.

You get the idea. Be honest: We have all traveled that road. To be angry when hurt is to be human. It is when you continue traveling that road, maybe even pitching a tent on the path's shoulder to relish the scenery, that resentment is able to send roots deep into your heart – and choke out your joy.

There was plenty of time and opportunity for Joseph to spiritually shuffle down a personal Resentment Highway, even as his body was driven along the desert caravan route to the Egyptian slave markets. Finally, he was jerked by his chains to stand before a crowd of strangers; he may have been stripped and displayed like livestock as the bids came in.

At the lowest point of Joseph's life, God was still in control. Joseph probably wondered if that was true, though the highest bidder turned out to be Potiphar, captain of the Egyptian Pharaoh's palace guard.

Joseph soon proved himself to Potiphar. This was no average household slave, the Egyptian aristocrat learned. Joseph excelled in all that he did. He was efficient, bright and creative in solutions to an increasing number of responsibilities. The young man had a positive attitude, too, about his work – always doing his best, not settling for "just enough" to avoid the whip, as other slaves did.

The Bible doesn't say how long it took Joseph to earn his trust, whether months or years, but his rise was nonetheless impressive:

"And his master saw that the LORD was with him and that the LORD made all he did to prosper in his hand. So Joseph found favor in his sight, and served him. Then he made him overseer of his house, and all that he had he put under his authority.

"So it was, from the time that he had made him overseer of his house and all that he had, that the LORD blessed the Egyptian's house for Joseph's sake; and the blessing of the LORD was on all that he had in the house and in the field.

"Thus he left all that he had in Joseph's hand, and he did not know what he had except for the bread which he ate . . ." (Genesis 39:3-6 NKJV)

I deliberately left out the last sentence of that final scripture because it tells us of another area in which the Lord has blessed Joseph. The lad was downright good-looking, and that was going to cause him some trouble. *Big* trouble.

"Now Joseph was handsome in form and appearance," the rest of Genesis 39:6 tells us. The slave-turned-overseer was not going unnoticed on the Potiphar household, and for more reasons than his management expertise.

Mrs. Potiphar herself had decided that while her husband was away, she would seduce the young man. He resisted; she persisted. She probably went shopping at the Nile branch of Victoria's Secret and poured on imported perfume. *"Sleep with me,"* Mrs. Potiphar begged. Joseph said *"no,"* time and time again.

"Look, my master does not know what is with me in the house, and he has committed all that he has to my hand. There is no one greater in this house than I, nor has he kept back anything from me but you, because you are his wife. How then can I do this great wickedness, and sin against God?"

(Genesis 39:8-9 NKJV)

Likely, this was not the first time Potiphar's wife had cheated on her husband. The pampered spouse of no less than the Captain of Pharaoh's Palace Guard *always* got what she wanted. She wanted Joseph, and by those animal-headed gods and goddesses she worshipped, she was going to add another notch to the bedpost.

A more direct approach was called for, she thought. If batting her eyelashes and increasingly more direct invitations would not work, well . . . one day, she just grabbed Joseph and demanded. To her surprise – and anger – the slave boy beat feet out of her clutches so fast he left part of his cloak behind, a ripped remnant still in her hand.

Like that, the scorned aristocratic woman's eagerness turned to rage, and a whopper of a lie. So, she screamed. As the other servants came running, she concocted a story of a barely escaped rape by that ungrateful Hebrew slave, Joseph. With a piece of his clothing in her hands as evidence, the tale sounded pretty convincing, too.

Convincing enough, in fact, that she told it again when Potiphar came home. The boss bought it, called his guards and off to prison Joseph went – once more tumbled from a position of favor by betrayal and lies.

Joseph had to wonder if heaven had gone crazy. He had gone from being Dad's favorite to being tossed into a pit, and then blessed to rise to trusted overseer in a fine house belonging to one of Egypt's elite.

And now, there he was, back in chains and back in a pit – deeper this time, and in the company of convicts whose only hope for freedom was usually execution. Joseph had landed in the Pharaoh's SuperMax prison.

Yes, this finally had to be the end. Once again, Joseph likely seethed in resentment toward those who had brought him so low – perhaps he even felt moments of resentment against God Himself.

Once again, he had nothing but the tattered clothes on his back. In the dark and breathing in the stink of his fellow inmates, the restraints chafed his ankles. But even there, Joseph found that flicker of hope: *the God of Abraham was still with him, regardless of the undeniably dire circumstances.*

It was not the end, he would learn; it was just the beginning.

Reflect: What are some thoughts from this chapter?

_____

_____

_____

_____

_____

_____

_____

_____

_____

Relate: How does this relate to your personal life and experiences?

_____

_____

_____

_____

_____

_____

Respond: Write a prayer to God asking for direction and help in these areas.

_____

_____

_____

_____

_____

_____

_____

_____

_____

_____

Chapter Three

It Takes More than Time to Heal Wounds of Resentment

ime heals all wounds? I don't believe that to be true. A little more than a year after helping my son, Chad, launch City Church in the Salt Lake Valley of Utah, the new congregation was solidly established and growing. From five families that trekked west from Wisconsin, hundreds were attending services. To this day, it continues to steadily grow, week in and week out.

As I write this in 2014, City Church regularly has around 700 in attendance at two Utah campuses, occasionally topping 1,000. Over the past few years, hundreds of people have made decisions to follow Christ. The vision that birthed the Utah ministry has been and will continue to be a great success.

But for me, the passage of time did not heal the wounds that continued to feed resentment within my thoughts, within my heart. The busy-ness of this season of ministry helped take my mind off of it for periods of time. I also relished my role as Director of Leadership and Church Expansion for Grace International, helping bring in independent churches and plant new congregations for this worldwide fellowship of evangelistic, Bible-believing Christians.

Time had, perhaps, dimmed the fury, but it was always there, just below the spiritual scar tissue.

Rose Kennedy, who endured the loss of *three* sons – Joe, shot down during World War II; then John, assassinated in Dallas when he was president; and finally, Robert, murdered as he campaigned for the White House – put it this way:

"It has been said, 'time heals all wounds.' I do not agree. The wounds remain. In time, the mind, protecting its sanity, covers them with scar tissue and the pain lessens. But it is never gone."

Time heals all wounds? I wasn't buying it, either. Now, had you said, *"Time wounds all heals,"* you might have gotten a loud and throaty "AMEN!" from me.

I believe Joseph found himself in a similar frame of mind. The scar tissue may have begun to come in over his wounds of the soul when he rose to favor in Potiphar's service, then ripped off to inflame the pain and memories anew when he was falsely accused and imprisoned.

"But the Lord was with Joseph and showed him mercy, and He gave him favor in the sight of the keeper of the prison.

"And the keeper of the prison committed to Joseph's hand all the prisoners who were in the prison; whatever they did there, it was his doing.

"The keeper of the prison did not look into anything that was under Joseph's authority, because the Lord was with him; and whatever he did, the Lord made it prosper." (Genesis 39:21-23 NJKV)

Consider that Joseph once again had to start from the bottom, this time with his reputation as surely in shreds as his coat of many colors. Word of his alleged dalliance with the wife of an important Egyptian noble followed him to prison, likely making him a special target for the jailer's wrath.

41

Not just a Hebrew slave; he had enraged one of the Pharaoh's Chosen. Where Joseph went was a place where the inmates seldom earned parole. Their terms were usually fatal: execution, after a prolonged, miserable stay of forced labor seasoned with the rod and the lash.

But you cannot keep a faithful man of God down. Even as he likely struggled with resentment, Joseph put his trust in the Lord and kept those dreams of destiny and heaven's favor. Opportunities came for Joseph to prove himself, including supervision of two new prize prisoners–the Pharaoh's chief baker and personal cupbearer.

These men who were responsible for what passed the Pharaoh's lips, had to have his complete trust. The Bible doesn't say how they offended him, but something had probably happened to spark his paranoia. Their lives were in limbo – and then came the dreams, troubling visions in the night.

They confided in Joseph: *"Do not interpretations belong to God? Tell them to me, please,"* he said.

You can read the details of those dreams, and their outcomes, in Genesis 40:8-22. In a nutshell, Joseph correctly predicted the cupbearer would be restored to his honored position, while the baker would end his days dangling from the gallows.

Joseph's hopes for getting out of the slammer rose with the release of the cupbearer. After all, this man had promised to take up Joseph's cause with the Pharaoh, proclaim his innocence to get this interpreter of dreams out of prison. Wham! Imagine Joseph's initial optimism, then worry and finally disappointment – and yes, more resentment – when he heard about the cupbearer's return to the court, and his silence about the Hebrew slave who foretold it all. Not a word.

Two more years in prison before God arranged events to remind – or convict – the cupbearer about that promise. Pharaoh was having dreams, disturbing ones, and none of his priests or fortunetellers could tell him what they meant. The cupbearer finally decided to open his mouth.

"I remember my faults this day," he confessed, and told the Pharaoh about Joseph and his 100 percent-accurate dream interpretations.

Finally, Joseph was sprung from the Big House. After washing off the smell of prison, getting a shave and some new clothes, the kid from Canaan, still only 30 years old, was hearing the most powerful ruler of his time spill his nightmares.

Genesis 41:9-46 recounts what happened next. Talk about one extreme to another. One moment he was in the pit of prison, his hope for release probably all but gone, and yet he was still faithful to God. Then probably in the space of a few hours, the Hebrew slave was second only to the Pharaoh in authority and honor.

Joseph, crediting God's revelation from the beginning, warned the Pharaoh of seven years of bounty to be followed by seven years of famine. He even offered some advice: Put away a fifth of the grain harvested each of those good years and store it for the lean years.

Brilliant idea Joseph, the Pharaoh said. And he knew right away who to put in charge. Not anyone at court, none of who could give him knowledge and peace, but this visionary foreigner:

"Inasmuch as God has shown you all this, there is no one as discerning and wise as you. You shall be over my house, and all my people shall be ruled according to your word; only in regard to the throne will I be greater than you." (Genesis 41:39-40 NKJV)

God had prepared the flow of time and events to free, bless and pour his favor upon Joseph. Victory was sweet, however long it had taken to obtain.

I believe it may have been at that moment – when Pharaoh literally put his signet ring on the former Hebrew slave's finger, giving him his authority – that Joseph felt whatever measure of resentment he had toward his brothers, and perhaps God, began to disintegrate.

Or at least that may have been the case to a large degree. While the pain and anger of resentment had certainly faded with Joseph's turn of fortune, his biggest test – and final triumph over the scars buried deep – was yet to come.

He didn't know it, but the past was about to make an abrupt entry into his life: the same brothers who betrayed him were on the way to Egypt.

Reflect: What are some thoughts from this chapter?

_____

_____

_____

_____

_____

_____

_____

_____

_____

Relate: How does this relate to your personal life and experiences?

_____

_____

_____

_____

_____

_____

_____

_____

Respond: Write a prayer to God asking for direction and help in these areas.

_____

_____

_____

_____

_____

_____

_____

_____

_____

_____

_____

Chapter Four

Beating Resentment: Choosing God's Way at Life's Crossroads

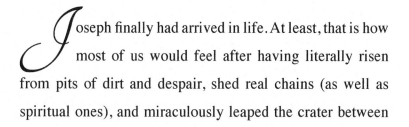

*J*oseph finally had arrived in life. At least, that is how most of us would feel after having literally risen from pits of dirt and despair, shed real chains (as well as spiritual ones), and miraculously leaped the crater between slave and prince.

At 30 years old, Joseph found himself recreated, at least in Pharaoh's mind, as *Zaphnath-Paaneah*. The meaning of the name ranges from *"savior of the world"* to the one most rabbinical scholars accept, *"he who revealed that which is hidden."* Either or both of those could apply. Through God's gifting, Joseph had revealed the meaning of Pharaoh's dreams, and his advice on how to act on those interpretations would "save" the Egyptian ruler's world from starvation and economic disaster.

As Joseph had prophesized, the seven years of plenty came. As Joseph's plan was implemented for storing away a fifth of each crop, harvests easily fed the nation and filled the granaries throughout Pharaoh's empire.

Joseph had great responsibilities, and by the time the seven years had passed, he also became a family man: the wife given to him by Pharaoh had born him two sons. As the abundance gave way to the foretold seven years of famine, his duties likely filled his days to the point where thoughts of home, his father and brothers faded.

There are biblical reasons to think so. Genesis 41:51-52 recounts that in naming his first-born Manasseh, Joseph declared that, *"For God has made me forget all my toil and all my father's house."* About his second-born, Ephraim, Joseph said, *"For God has caused me to be fruitful in the land of my affliction."*

Day by day, Joseph oversaw the distribution of the food stores to feed the hungry. As the famine spread, caravans came from neighboring lands, and often Joseph presided over the negotiations. The carefully hoarded grain went out;

the treasuries of the Pharaoh swelled with gold, silver, gems and other goods.

Then one day, Joseph found it was his brothers who were bowing at his feet, begging for food. This was the same brood that had fallen upon him, roughed him up, tossed him into a cistern and then sold him into slavery all those years ago.

As they groveled at his feet, not recognizing this powerful Egyptian official as the brother they had so cruelly betrayed, the embers of resentment must have glowed, maybe even flared into a desire for payback.

Then Joseph remembered the dreams that had gotten him into such trouble with his brothers: those sheaves of grain, the stars, and bowing to the kid with the amazing coat of many colors. And here they were, faces to the floor – at his mercy.

Perhaps the desire for revenge fought with his love for his long-lost family, however bruised the relationship had been. Whatever the case, there was no swift justice, no lopped off heads rolling in the sand. Still, Joseph wanted to know the hearts of his brothers.

He questioned them, even using an interpreter as he played the part of a suspicious Egyptian leader, accusing them of being spies. Their knees were knocking. *"Brothers, we're toast! This guy is going to either kills us or throw us in the dungeons for the rest of our lives,"* they probably whispered to each other.

Finally, Joseph declared that he would hold one of them hostage while the rest went back to Canaan with the grain they had purchased. Then the hardest demand: they could not return without their youngest brother, Benjamin.

Eventually, they did return with Benjamin, with Jacob's reluctant approval. Joseph subjected his brothers to more tests, and then, finally, he was satisfied. In tears, he revealed himself: *"I am Joseph, your brother, whom you sold into Egypt."*

By this time, Joseph had won his battle with resentment. Forgiveness flowed from him as he quickly added, *"But now, do not therefore be grieved or angry with yourselves because you sold me here; for God sent me before you to preserve life. . . . It was not you who sent me here, but God."* (Genesis 45:4-5, 8 NKJV)

Where Joseph arrived in *his* battle with resentment is where we *all* need to be in our own struggles. We have to let go of betrayal, hurt, anger and the desire for revenge and embrace forgiveness.

Like Joseph, defeating resentment takes more than letting go of the darkness and rage. To forgive is more than a state of mind – it requires action. Joseph gave up his "right" to exact revenge when he had the opportunity, and he went further, reaching out to heal the rift with his brothers.

For me, that pivotal moment of decision came in early 2013, and it came out of the blue.

One day as I checked my e-mail, there was a message from the pastor of a large church in Durban, South Africa. It turned out that the very same minister who had pulled my retirement funding, and the financial support promised for the new Utah ministry, was in Africa and had approached the Durban pastor about holding a seminar in his church.

This minister's marriage seminars had been very successful and popular. His sharp sense of humor and charisma were very well received. Jan and I had been among his biggest fans; however, that was before the broken promises and before the resentment began to take root. Although the work in Utah had proven successful despite having the financial rug pulled out from under us, the temptation to exact a measure of revenge rose up like a flame rekindled from nearly extinguished coals when I read that e-mail.

The South African pastor told me in the e-mail that if I said the word, he wouldn't let the minister use their building for his seminars. I am ashamed to admit it, but my initial thought was, *"Well, buddy, I could cost you some serious money just by saying, 'no.' I could torpedo this."*

Thank God, it was only for a moment I considered it. But I knew this was a critical test for me. Would I allow the Holy Spirit's work of healing, forgiveness and renewed purpose in my heart go up in restoked flames of resentment?

No, I would not, I decided. Instantly, I finally felt completely free of the past bitterness. *"Get thee behind me Satan!"* I thought, and then e-mailed him back. I not only gave my blessing but also praised this minister's seminars, assuring the Durban pastor that hosting them would be a blessing to his congregation.

Let me offer just a couple examples, in one case from a famous Christian, and another from an unheralded grief-stricken mother, that far more eloquently show the miracle of forgiveness and defeat of resentment than my own story.

The late Corrie ten Boom's best-selling book, *The Hiding Place* (also made into a critically-acclaimed movie), told about her Dutch Christian family's suffering for sheltering Jews from the Nazis during World War II. She lost her father and sister to Hitler's concentration camps, where she too had experienced cruelty and deprivation first-hand.

Corrie ten Boom had every reason to hate the Nazis. Yet after the war ended, she became an evangelist for the gospel, speaking in churches throughout Europe about God's forgiveness. Those appearances eventually took her to a Munich church in the heart of Germany.

In a 1972 article in Guideposts Magazine, she wrote about meeting a former guard from one of the camps where she had been held. Corrie ten Boom immediately recognized the man as a prison camp guard. After the service, he approached her, his hand out.

"A fine message, Fraulein! How good it is to know that, as you say, all our sins are at the bottom of the sea!" he said.

Corrie ten Boom admitted that initially, rather than taking her former tormentor's hand, she rummaged through her purse. *"I was face to face with one of my captors, and my blood seemed to freeze,"* she wrote.

The man, who had not remembered her as one of his prisoners, recounted how he had been a guard at the same camp she talked about, Ravensbruck. Since then, however, he had become a Christian. Now, his hand out once more, he plaintively asked for her forgiveness.

"I wrestled with the most difficult thing I had ever had to do," she wrote, recounting how she struggled with painful memories of her lost loved ones and her own nightmarish experiences . . . then prayed for strength to forgive.

"And so woodenly, mechanically, I thrust my hand into the one stretched out to me. And as I did, an incredible thing took place. The current started in my shoulder, raced down my arm, sprang into our joined hands. And then this healing warmth seemed to flood my whole being, bringing tears to my eyes.

As Corrie ten Boom forgave, she said, *"I had never known God's love so intensely, as I did then."*

Then there is the remarkable story of Mary Johnson, a Minneapolis woman whose 20-year-old son, her only son, had been shot to death at a party in 1993. His killer was a 16-year-old street punk. As she told CBS News correspondent Steve Hartman, all she wanted was justice in the form of revenge: *"He was an animal. He deserved to be caged,"* she said.

The teenage killer, Oshea Israel, was caged, sentenced to more than 25 years in prison. Then, after serving 17 of those years, he was paroled . . . not only back to Minneapolis, but in what otherwise might seem a cruel turn of fate, he moved into an apartment one door down from Mary Johnson. This was, in fact, a model of incredible mercy and forgiveness.

Mary Johnson had arranged to visit her son's killer in prison a few years prior to him moving into her apartment complex. Her mission was to find some way to follow Christ's command to forgive. One visit turned into regular meetings, and when he got out, Mary helped clear the way for him to move into the unit next to her own.

"Unforgiveness is like a cancer. It will eat you from the inside out," she told Hartman. *"Me forgiving him does not diminish what he's done. Yes, he murdered my son – but the forgiveness is for me."*

As for Oshea Israel, he confessed he was still working on forgiving himself – even as he sings in church and preaches about forgiveness to audiences in both the pews and in prisons.

The battle with resentment can be won. God is the undeniable catalyst. It worked for Joseph, for me, for Corrie ten Boom, for Mary Johnson – and Oshea Israel.

Why not you?

Reflect: What are some thoughts from this chapter?

_____

_____

_____

_____

_____

_____

_____

_____

_____

_____

Relate: How does this relate to your personal life and experiences?

_____

_____

_____

_____

_____

_____

_____

Respond: Write a prayer to God asking for direction and help in these areas.

_____

_____

_____

_____

_____

_____

_____

_____

_____

Chapter Five

Resentment:
A Double-Edged Sword

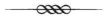

The 16ᵗʰ Century English poet John Donne put it this way:

> *"No man is an island,*
>
> *Entire of itself,*
>
> *Every man is a piece of the continent,*
>
> *A part of the main."*

No doubt, Donne, also an Anglican churchman, was familiar with the writings of the Apostle Paul. Donne's famous, oft-quoted poem *"No Man is an Island,"* certainly echoes what Paul wrote more than 1,500 years before in his letter to the believers in Rome:

"For none of us lives to himself, and no one dies to himself. For if we live, we live to the Lord; and if we die, we die to the Lord. Therefore, whether we live or die, we are the Lord's. For to this end Christ died and rose and lived again, that He might be Lord of both the dead and the living." (Romans 14:7-9 NKJV)

Donne concluded with the idea that love transcends self-interest, that *"Any man's death diminishes me, because I am involved in mankind . . ."* Paul would have agreed, but likely reminded Donne that in the equality of love, our ultimate purpose is Christ – in this world and the next.

There is an underlying principle, however far you take the words. We do not live, act or suffer alone. That is also true when it comes to resentment. Like the ripples of a stone in a pond, how you and I deal with hurt, unforgiveness and bitterness affects our loved ones, friends and co-workers.

In this book so far, I have shared how my resentment affected me, and how it affected Joseph and others like Corrie ten Boom and a grieving Minneapolis mother. Like an atomic blast, the damage is not all in the explosion and the mushroom cloud that forms instantly afterward.

There is the fallout. That ash that rains down in the hours and days following the blast, sickening and either killing people outright or shortening the lives of those with radiation-caused cancers.

In my struggle with bitterness, I was so focused on my own pain and anger that I did not realize at first how it was affecting my own family and associates in Utah. For a time, as Jan and I saw our savings disappear to support the Salt Lake City work and pastoral salaries, I even felt some resentment towards them, thinking that our sacrifices were not being fully appreciated.

That was not true; I have since made amends with my children and other pastoral associates I offended – not by outright mistreatment, but in my unspoken attitude toward them during those dark moments. Still, I did not know – until I asked them to share with me – what my family was going through because of what I was experiencing.

My daughter, Brooke, who is married to the City Church Worship Pastor, Josh Pierce, wrote that she and my son-in-law suffered, too. It humbled me to see how she and Josh, as well as my son, City Church Lead Pastor Chad Jacobson and his wife, Amanda, handled it all.

"I personally experienced the high cost of resentment when I carried over my parents' hurt and pain into my life. They went through a very difficult season, and it was so hard for me to watch them go through it. I let it eat away at my spirit, so much so that I asked God on numerous occasions to let me feel the hurt instead of them, especially the hurt my dad was dealing with," Brooke wrote.

"I truly believed it would have been easier on me. Nothing prepared me, as a daughter, to watch my parents go through betrayal and to be treated so unfairly when they had dedicated their lives to making a Godly difference. My dad, who had always been a strong and confident man in my life, was slowly beginning to be overwhelmed with sadness, regret, and defeat. I felt angry and resentful."

The kids may have been a little slower to get past the resentment than Jan and I were, but not by much. Brooke says they gave it all to God and allowed the Holy Spirit to heal their hurt for us with a balm of peace and forgiveness.

"[The experience] also encouraged me to hold that same line of thinking in every area of my life, with every person I deal with. I even came up with a code word to remind me: 'balloon,' as in 'let it go.'"

Brooke, Josh, Chad and Amanda decided to follow the advice in 1 Peter 5:7 to *"Cast all [their] cares upon God."* Brooke concludes by saying there was freedom in such trust, a release that allowed her to *"choose to not let resentment have a place in my life anymore."* Such an attitude is a perfect reflection of another of Paul's observations:

"And we know that all things work together for good to those who love God, to those who are the called according to His purpose." (Romans 8:28 NKJV)

How about when the source of resentment . . . *is you?*

Some years ago, I personally had the painful task of parting ministerial ways with an extremely talented Music and Worship Associate Pastor. I had known Matt Perkins for many years, and we had developed a very close friendship – almost that of a father and son.

Matt and his wife Marybeth had been a blessing to our former church in Wisconsin, but he felt called to take a position in California. It did not work out, and we welcomed him back to his former duties in Green Bay. But after a few years, it just wasn't working for either of us; telling him the bad news was one of the toughest things I have ever had to do.

I felt we had parted as friends, but the emotional fallout and pain could not help but birth resentment. Again, how Matt eventually let the resentment go not only showed him to truly be a man of God, but also left me with a fusion of loving pride and humility.

After enduring and conquering his own battle with resentment, Matt went on to minister in Florida at one of the largest Assemblies of God churches in the nation. He puts it this way:

"Unbelief, fear, embarrassment, rejection, anger . . . where do I go from here? These were all thoughts and emotions that were rapidly going through my mind," he wrote about the moments after we met that day.

"It hit me a few minutes into our conversation that this amazing season of ministry in our lives had come to an end. The future was cloudy, and we asked ourselves how our kids would respond to this change — in fact, how would we even tell them?

"So much of our lives had been wrapped up in the church in Green Bay. Would we find a new church community where we would again feel at home? For a time, I even wondered if

I wanted to serve on a church staff again . . . but God opened the door for us to minister Orlando, Florida," Matt recalled.

It was during a worship leaders' conference in Houston in 2009 that Matt says he realized unresolved feelings stemming from his Green Bay departure was robbing him of the joy he wanted to experience in his new role.

"Here I had a position as a Worship Pastor in a very large, well-respected church, and I couldn't force myself to be happy. Then during one of the sessions, I felt the Holy Spirit telling me to go and call Arni Jacobson and thank him for his investment in my life!"

In prayer, Matt says he tried to assure God that he held no resentment, that the negative feelings had been dealt with, and that he and Marybeth had moved on. But the Holy Spirit was persistent. If, as Matt insisted, he truly held no resentment over the way things had ended in Green Bay, there should be no reason not to tell me that directly.

"At that point, I knew that I had to speak with [Arni]," Matt wrote. *"I quickly left the conference, went back to my hotel and placed the phone call. I was nervous because it had been over two years since Arni and I had spoken; I didn't even know if he would take my call."*

Matt confessed that he hoped, just a bit, that his call would go to my voice mail. No such luck. When I answered the phone, Matt cleared his throat and began, *"Hello, Arni? You probably didn't expect to get a phone call from me today. I just wanted to thank you for your investment in my life and apologize if I offended you when everything came to an end in Green Bay."* Matt followed through, and both of us, with a renewed friendship, are glad he did.

For me, there was gratitude for his positive attitude, and an elder mentor's satisfaction in the maturity of this young man who had triumphed over what he could have seen as a setback.

Matt wrote that the call was *"not only a relief to have been obedient to God, but also to begin repairing a relationship with someone who, for a number of years, had treated me like his son."*

When he called Marybeth at their home in Orlando, he learned God had also given his wife the same desire to mend our two families' relationship. While Matt was making his call, Marybeth had gone out to buy a card for my wife, Jan.

To this day, Matt marvels over the Holy Spirit's leading in their lives and the healing purpose He worked in their hearts and ours.

"Prior to that call, I honestly didn't feel that I was holding in any resentment towards Arni. However, the peace that I felt following that conversation was undeniable. For the next several days, God continued to break me and speak to my heart in such a unique way.

"As I look back on that week in Houston, I can say without a doubt that I was changed. I wasn't worried about being the one who was 'right' in the situation. I let it go and as a result, God restored a treasured relationship," Matt said.

He has advice for anyone struggling with resentment: forgive, reach out in healing and love, and let it go.

Matt asks, *"What phone calls do you need to make today? Are there people or events that when you think about them you automatically cringe? It's time to release them and yourself from whatever happened."*

Matt concludes, *"Celebrate the people that God has brought into your life. Honor them and thank them for the value that they bring to your life."*

I could not have said it better myself.

Reflect: What are some thoughts from this chapter?

_____

_____

_____

_____

_____

_____

_____

_____

_____

Relate: How does this relate to your personal life and experiences?

_____

_____

_____

_____

_____

_____

_____

Respond: Write a prayer to God asking for direction and help in these areas.

_____

_____

_____

_____

_____

_____

_____

_____

_____

_____

Chapter Six

The Other Side of Resentment: Forgiven, but Can You Forgive Yourself?

Seventeen years had passed since Joseph brought his father Jacob, his brothers and their families, flocks and herds across the Sinai Desert to take refuge in Egypt from drought and starvation.

In the rich pasture lands of Goshen, Joseph's shepherd brothers thrived, and the numbers of their livestock and children were growing. In the peace and plenty of the present, the sins of the past seemed to have been buried.

However, it would prove to be a shallow grave. When Jacob died, the winds of guilt and memory exposed that betrayal of so long ago. It was fear that brought it back to life:

Joseph's brothers were convinced that with the old man dead, nothing would stand in the way of Joseph settling accounts.

They had plenty of time to worry about it, too. The whole family, escorted by members of Pharaoh's Court, made the long journey to Canaan to bury Jacob. There had been seven days of mourning, and then they made the long trek back to Egypt.

Each step closer to Goshen must have been loaded with dread for the brothers; maybe they imagined how the same desert crossing must have been for Joseph, in chains. . . and wondered if they might get to find out first-hand.

"Perhaps Joseph will hate us, and may actually repay us for all the evil we did to him," they muttered to each other (Genesis 50:15 NKJV).

A desperate strategy emerged. The brothers sent a message to Joseph, claiming that the patriarch had told them he wanted Joseph to forgive the boys for what they had done.

After allowing the message time to take root, the brothers showed up, fell down at his feet and waited – for mercy or for the axe to fall. Literally, perhaps.

They got mercy and tears. Joseph wept when he realized that despite his years of showing love and care for his brothers, they were still in fear of him. Joseph knew he had dealt with his resentment long ago, but his brothers couldn't understand how that had been possible.

"Do not be afraid, for am I in the place of God? You meant evil against me; but God meant it for good, to bring it about as it is this day, to save many people alive." (Genesis 50:19-20 NKJV)

Joseph renewed his promise to provide for his brothers and their children. The Bible says he *comforted* and *spoke kindly* to them. I like to imagine a big group hug took place — all of Jacob's sons truly together, at last.

While Joseph had let go of his resentment and completely forgiven his brothers, they had not dealt with the other side of the resentment coin: the guilt of those who brought it about to begin with. Receiving forgiveness is hard, especially when you cannot forgive yourself.

Things worked out for Joseph and his brothers. Those families became a nation that brought the love of God to the world through Jesus, a descendant of the Jewish King David. We are blessed today because thousands of years ago, a betrayed slave-boy-turned-Egyptian viceroy chose to forgive – to let his resentment go.

Resentment has become no less a problem for believers today. Indeed, it is a worldwide spiritual epidemic. Worst of all, it thrives and ruins lives and testimonies among Christians – the very people who should be examples to the world of forgiveness in action.

Resentment births retaliation, robs us of our sleep, breaks up businesses, splinters families and ruins churches. In the Body of Christ, it derails congregational harmony, lurking like a disease just below the spiritual and emotional surface for millions of believers.

Some Christians may even be able to argue with unassailable conviction that the target of their resentment is 100 percent guilty; they *deserve* it!

Surely, that is how the angry crowd must have felt when they dragged the adulteress – caught in the act, no doubt about her guilt – before Jesus and demanded she be stoned to death, as provided in the Law of Moses.

John 8:1-11 recounts what happened. Jesus did not argue that the woman was wrongly accused, for surely she was not. Instead, " . . . *Jesus stooped down and wrote on the ground with His finger, as though He did not hear.*

"So when they continued asking Him, He raised Himself up and said to them, 'He who is without sin among you, let

him throw a stone at her first.' And again He stooped down and wrote on the ground."

I would love to know what Jesus wrote. Some scholars speculate that he wrote down the names of the woman's accusers and their own sins. Others surmise he was mimicking His Father's act of writing the Ten Commandments on stone tablets, thousands of years before.

Whatever the words, we can be sure they came down to the same meaning: Forgiven.

The scripture tells us that following the thumping of stones as they fell on the ground, the woman's accusers left. Finally, the only ones left were Jesus and the woman.

"When Jesus had raised Himself up and saw no one but the woman, He said to her, 'Woman, where are those accusers of yours? Has no one condemned you?' She said, 'No one, Lord.'

"And Jesus said to her, 'Neither do I condemn you; go and sin no more.'"

She was guilty. Under the Law, she deserved to die. We are guilty too, and without the blood of Christ, we also stand condemned. Bottom line: there is no room for resentment in the heart of God's children.

After all, if Jesus wrote your name in the sands of this present time, what sins would be listed next to it? So, drop those stones . . . of resentment!

How do we conquer resentment? Is there a magical Twelve-Step program? A particularly blessed pill? Will being anointed with oil do it?

Well, you don't *conquer* it. You have to **let it go**. Pray for the Holy Spirit to help you shed the chains of resentment that are enslaving you. Here are some steps to help you walk away, not looking back:

1. Acknowledge your feelings of resentment; admit its effects on you, your relationships with your loved ones, friends and God. You need the attitude of David, expressed in Psalm 139:23-24: *"Search me, O God, and know my heart; Try me, and know my anxieties; And see if there is any wicked way in me, And lead me in the way everlasting."* Admit, seek, and give forgiveness.

2. Realize that in that trial, betrayal, loss or setback you experienced, *God was positioning you for greatness.* Romans 8:28 is your promise of this: *"And we know*

that all things work together for good to those who love God, to those who are the called according to His purpose."

3. Make a step toward the altar to confirm your desire for freedom from resentment through the Holy Spirit. This can be a response in your church (going forward physically) or during your personal prayer time. Either way, though, be accountable — *share* your prayer and commitment with a pastor or other trusted believer.

4. Someone has to own it; someone has to step up. Do your best to make it right. This may be the toughest thing to do, but the act of forgiveness alone will not repair broken relationships or heal wounds suffered or inflicted in retaliation by you. Forgiveness must be sought and expressed.

5. There are no guarantees, of course, that your efforts will be accepted. If they are, a relationship will have been restored – it likely will be even better than it was before whatever occurred to damage it.

In this book's final chapter, I will share how that final, painful and yet liberating step came about for me.

Reflect: What are some thoughts from this chapter?

_____

_____

_____

_____

_____

_____

_____

_____

_____

Relate: How does this relate to your personal life and experiences?

_____

_____

_____

_____

_____

_____

_____

Respond: Write a prayer to God asking for direction and help in these areas.

_____

_____

_____

_____

_____

_____

_____

_____

_____

Chapter Seven

Climbing the
Summit of Mount Resentment

*I*n my heart, I had known for years that my victory over resentment would not be complete until I had reached out to the man I had blamed as being the catalyst for years of sometimes painful, though ultimately enlightening and liberating lessons about forgiving – and being forgiven.

It just never seemed to be the right time, or maybe I convinced myself that was the case. In the end, that trip to my iPad to write an e-mail to my former associate and ministerial successor in Wisconsin seemed like the longest I had ever taken.

I'm not kidding. I literally ended up going around the world, to a pastoral conference in India, before I finally found myself ready. While praying in an upper room at a Christian college amid the humidity of August 2013, and later while waiting to speak to other believers about the curse of resentment, I had special times of listening to the Holy Spirit.

My mind was clear; my spirit focused. At one point, I asked my host if the mosquitoes in India carried malaria, a deadly disease that continues to claim millions of lives each year. *"Not at this altitude,"* he assured me.

I smiled to myself. Resentment is a lot like malaria, it seemed. It dawned on me that to overcome the bitter root of unforgiveness, we must *move to a higher spiritual altitude!*

I had to make that ascent before I could plant any flags on Mount Resentment. I jotted down what came to me next:

"I must apologize to my former associate about how I reacted to what seemed to be, at the time, devastating news for me and my family."

Oh, boy. I remembered, ashamed, how when the funding for retirement and the Utah work had been pulled, I had decided not to wait to see if he, as indicated, might have worked to eventually restore those commitments. He had even started with a partial payment of what had been earlier promised – but after a few months *I* refused to receive even that.

Resentment will blind you to a different path and cripple restoration of relationships if you surrender to it. For a time, I did. I am also convinced it dimmed my spiritual vision, too, until I pleaded with God to help me lay it all at His feet.

About sixty-five years ago, polio was an epidemic, crippling and often killing millions of people around the world. Then in the early 1950s, a vaccine developed by Dr. Jonas Salk effectively brought this dreaded disease to its knees.

The vaccine for resentment, a spiritual epidemic with potentially eternal consequences, is forgiving, and receiving forgiveness! That was my message that day in India, and when I finished speaking to those 40 or so pastors, every single one of them came to the altar to lay their resentment down at the feet of Christ.

Watching those ministers of God allowing the Holy Spirit to break the bonds of anger, unforgiveness and unhealed wounds of the soul, I was anxious to take my own final step – to reach that summit. I breathed a prayer and began typing this e-mail:

"Here it goes. I want to spend a few moments in this e-mail apologizing to you, and [your church] family.

"I am writing a new book titled, 'The High Cost of Resentment' and how I was set free. As you are painfully aware, a lot of stuff happened on my departure from [my former church].

"First, I moved too quickly and put you and your leadership in a very difficult financial position. Second, as my resentment grew I did not wait for you or the church to recover. Then when you did begin to pay me, I was so full of resentment that I quit taking the money.

"Third, I have come to realize that I need to own the whole situation, and never again point any accusatory verbiage at you.

"As in the Bible [end of the Gospel of John] it says the volume of the book could not contain what Jesus did, neither could an e-mail touch every issue. I am humbly asking for your forgiveness.

"I guess I could understand if you refuse, but I'm praying you will find it in your heart to forgive me. You can use this e-mail anyway you see fit. Share it with your staff, family, and, if you desire, read it to the church.

"Jan and I are still proud of you and your wide-reaching ministry.

"God Bless, and continued blessings on your life and ministry. . . ."

Less than a half an hour after I hit "send," Jan and I were both in tears as my former associate's gracious, loving response arrived in my inbox. I read, in part:

"Dear Arni, I want to you know that forgiveness is not needed because we hold no ill will towards you. But to the extent that you have asked for it, I freely give it.

"This separation has been awkward and difficult for me. I was just telling some people yesterday, as I have done often, that I would not be in ministry today if it were not for you. You were the only mentor in my life that believed enough in me and encouraged me to start to preach and teach."

He went on to praise God for the thousands of lives, marriages and families saved and enriched by his ministry – and thanked me for having faith in him early and encouraging him *"to be the person God made me to be."*

He confessed to *"a sense of sadness knowing that we were not on good terms. To clear this up would be a great blessing to me."*

In closing, he expressed regret for how things had gone south with the funding those many years ago.

"Certainly, we would all do it differently if we had the chance. While there were disagreements, I don't believe anyone intended evil.

"Is there anything I can do at this point?"

For both of us, it was the beginning of renewing a special relationship, of healing wounds that two brothers in the faith should never have had to endure in the first place. I took full responsibility for my part in that.

Since then, we have spent time talking, both on the phone and in person, and restoring our relationship. We are even looking into future ministry endeavors together.

For both of us, the words of Paul so long ago have taken on a freshness that has never smelled sweeter:

"And we know that all things work together for good to those who love God, to those who are the called according to His purpose." (Romans 8:28 NKJV)

This book will be read by Christians and non-believers alike. As I wrote earlier, resentment affects us all.

But the healing that began with that e-mail exchange between my former associate and myself, and for many others who have restored relationships through letting go resentment and embracing forgiveness, had a firm foundation: faith in Christ.

If you have not accepted Jesus as your Savior, I invite you to do that right now. It is a journey that begins with a simple prayer:

"Lord Jesus, I know I'm a sinner; I am not where I want to be, and I ask Your forgiveness. I believe that Jesus died on the cross to pay the price for my sins. Wash me clean from all sin, shame, and guilt. Come into my life as my Lord and Savior. In Your Name, I consider it done. Amen."

Next, find and faithfully attend a good Bible-believing and preaching church. This is a critical part of growing in faith, as you both receive love and teaching to help to walk in the light of Christ.

As Martin Luther King Jr. once said, *"Darkness cannot drive out darkness; only light can do that. Hate cannot drive out hate; only love can do that."*

Walking in the light, free of the burden of resentment, is God's will for all of His children.

Reflect: What are some thoughts from this chapter?

_____

_____

_____

_____

_____

_____

_____

_____

Relate: How does this relate to your personal life and experiences?

_____

_____

_____

_____

_____

_____

Respond: Write a prayer to God asking for direction and help in these areas.

_____

_____

_____

_____

_____

_____

_____

_____

_____

_____

_____

30 Days to Freedom Challenge

Day 1 – Resentment can come from many different situations – hurt, betrayal, disappointments, and many more. Do you hold any resentment in your life? Write about it.

_____

_____

_____

_____

_____

_____

_____

_____

_____

_____

_____

_____

_____

_____

_____

_____

_____

_____

_____

_____

Praise / Prayer:

_____

_____

_____

_____

_____

_____

_____

_____

_____

Verse for this section: "Get rid of all bitterness, rage and anger, brawling and slander, along with every form of malice. Be kind and compassionate to one another, forgiving each other, just as in Christ God forgave you." –Ephesians 4:31-32 NIV

Day 2 – Have you ever been treated unfairly? Been accused of false motives? Felt you didn't get what you deserved? Experienced broken promises? What happened? How did it feel?

_____

_____

_____

_____

_____

_____

_____

_____

_____

_____

_____

_____

_____

_____

_____

_____

_____

Praise / Prayer:

_____

_____

_____

_____

_____

_____

_____

_____

_____

_____

Verse for this section: "Get rid of all bitterness, rage and anger, brawling and slander, along with every form of malice. Be kind and compassionate to one another, forgiving each other, just as in Christ God forgave you." –Ephesians 4:31-32 NIV

Day 3 – Take a minute to praise God for the good things in your life.

_____

_____

_____

_____

_____

_____

_____

_____

_____

_____

_____

_____

_____

_____

_____

_____

_____

Praise / Prayer:

_____

_____

_____

_____

_____

_____

_____

_____

_____

_____

_____

_____

Verse for this section: "Get rid of all bitterness, rage and anger, brawling and slander, along with every form of malice. Be kind and compassionate to one another, forgiving each other, just as in Christ God forgave you." –Ephesians 4:31-32 NIV

Day 4 – Oftentimes resentment can foster side effects in your life, such as physical illness, anger, and depression. What side effects have you seen from unforgiveness and resentment in your own life?

_____

_____

_____

_____

_____

_____

_____

_____

_____

_____

_____

_____

_____

_____

_____

_____

_____

_____

Praise / Prayer:

_____

_____

_____

_____

_____

_____

_____

_____

_____

_____

Verse for this section: "Get rid of all bitterness, rage and anger, brawling and slander, along with every form of malice. Be kind and compassionate to one another, forgiving each other, just as in Christ God forgave you." –Ephesians 4:31-32 NIV

Day 5 – Read Mark 11:25 and write it below. What does this verse tell you about forgiving others?

_____

_____

_____

_____

_____

_____

_____

_____

_____

_____

_____

_____

_____

_____

_____

_____

_____

_____

Praise / Prayer:

_____

_____

_____

_____

_____

_____

_____

_____

_____

_____

_____

Verse for this section: "Get rid of all bitterness, rage and anger, brawling and slander, along with every form of malice. Be kind and compassionate to one another, forgiving each other, just as in Christ God forgave you." –Ephesians 4:31-32 NIV

Day 6 – When you feel upset, how to you handle it? Do you get angry or sad? Do you talk to someone? Do you talk to God?

_____

_____

_____

_____

_____

_____

_____

_____

_____

_____

_____

_____

_____

_____

_____

_____

_____

Praise / Prayer:

_____

_____

_____

_____

_____

_____

_____

_____

_____

_____

Verse for this section: "Get rid of all bitterness, rage and anger, brawling and slander, along with every form of malice. Be kind and compassionate to one another, forgiving each other, just as in Christ God forgave you." –Ephesians 4:31-32 NIV

Day 7 – Sometimes it can hurt worse to have someone you love going through a difficult time. We may even try to control the situation or fix it for them. Have you ever taken on a loved one's offense?

_____

_____

_____

_____

_____

_____

_____

_____

_____

_____

_____

_____

_____

_____

_____

_____

_____

_____

_____

Praise / Prayer:

_____

_____

_____

_____

_____

_____

_____

_____

_____

_____

_____

_____

Verse for this section: "Get rid of all bitterness, rage and anger, brawling and slander, along with every form of malice. Be kind and compassionate to one another, forgiving each other, just as in Christ God forgave you." –Ephesians 4:31-32 NIV

Day 8 – Talk about the story of Joseph (Genesis 37-50). How might you have acted if you were put in the same situation? What can this teach us about patience and forgiveness?

_____

_____

_____

_____

_____

_____

_____

_____

_____

_____

_____

_____

_____

_____

_____

_____

_____

_____

_____

_____

Praise / Prayer:

_____

_____

_____

_____

_____

_____

_____

_____

_____

_____

Verse for this section: "Get rid of all bitterness, rage and anger, brawling and slander, along with every form of malice. Be kind and compassionate to one another, forgiving each other, just as in Christ God forgave you." –Ephesians 4:31-32 NIV

Day 9 – Read James 5:16 and write it below. Why is it important that we talk to others about our unforgiveness or hurts?

_____

_____

_____

_____

_____

_____

_____

_____

_____

_____

_____

_____

_____

_____

Praise / Prayer:

_____

_____

_____

_____

_____

_____

_____

_____

_____

_____

Verse for this section: "Get rid of all bitterness, rage and anger, brawling and slander, along with every form of malice. Be kind and compassionate to one another, forgiving each other, just as in Christ God forgave you." –Ephesians 4:31-32 NIV

Day 10 – Write about a time where God helped you through a difficult situation or relationship. Remember that God is always there for you. Spend some time thanking God for bringing you through the hard times.

_____

_____

_____

_____

_____

_____

_____

_____

_____

_____

_____

_____

_____

_____

_____

_____

_____

Praise / Prayer:

_____

_____

_____

_____

_____

_____

_____

_____

_____

Now it's your turn! Write out Ephesians 4:31-32 NIV:

_____

_____

_____

_____

Day 11 – Oftentimes our resentment is linked to our inability to express our emotions outwardly. Do you have someone in your life that you can talk to about your struggles? Write that person's name down and also the things you would like to talk with them about. Make it a priority to set up a time to talk with them this week.

_____

_____

_____

_____

_____

_____

_____

_____

_____

_____

_____

_____

_____

_____

_____

_____

_____

_____

_____

_____

_____

Praise / Prayer:

_____

_____

_____

_____

_____

_____

_____

_____

_____

Verse for this section: "I do not consider myself yet to have taken hold of it. But one thing I do: Forgetting what is behind and straining toward what is ahead, I press on toward the goal to win the prize for which God has called me heavenward in Christ Jesus." –Philippians 3:13-14 NIV

Day 12 – Charles Swindoll once wrote, *"The longer I live, the more I realize the impact of attitude on life. Attitude, to me, is more important than facts. It is more important than the past, than education, than money, than circumstances, than failure, than successes, than what other people think or say or do. It is more important than appearance, giftedness or skill. It will make or break a company... a church... a home. The remarkable thing is we have a choice everyday regarding the attitude we will embrace for that day. We cannot change our past... we cannot change the fact that people will act in a certain way. We cannot change the inevitable. The only thing we can do is play on the one string we have, and that is our attitude. I am convinced that life is 10% what happens to me and 90% how I react to it. And so it is with you... we are in charge of our attitudes."* What does this mean to you (especially the last two sentences)?

_____

_____

_____

_____

_____

_____

_____

_____

_____

_____

_____

_____

_____

_____

_____

_____

_____

_____

_____

_____

_____

Praise / Prayer:

_____

_____

_____

_____

_____

_____

_____

_____

_____

_____

Verse for this section: "I do not consider myself yet to have taken hold of it. But one thing I do: Forgetting what is behind and straining toward what is ahead, I press on toward the goal to win the prize for which God has called me heavenward in Christ Jesus." –Philippians 3:13-14 NIV

Day 13 – Negativity can be very present in a lot of peoples' lives, and negativity can hang on tight to feelings of resentment. Do you feel that you are generally a negative person or a positive person? Explain.

_____

_____

_____

_____

_____

_____

_____

_____

_____

_____

_____

_____

_____

_____

_____

_____

_____

_____

_____

Praise / Prayer:

_____

_____

_____

_____

_____

_____

_____

_____

_____

_____

_____

Verse for this section: "I do not consider myself yet to have taken hold of it. But one thing I do: Forgetting what is behind and straining toward what is ahead, I press on toward the goal to win the prize for which God has called me heavenward in Christ Jesus." –Philippians 3:13-14 NIV

Day 14 – There is a saying that "time heals all wounds." Do you believe this is true? Why or why not?

_____

_____

_____

_____

_____

_____

_____

_____

_____

_____

_____

_____

_____

_____

_____

_____

_____

_____

_____

_____

Praise / Prayer:

_____

_____

_____

_____

_____

_____

_____

_____

_____

_____

Verse for this section: "I do not consider myself yet to have taken hold of it. But one thing I do: Forgetting what is behind and straining toward what is ahead, I press on toward the goal to win the prize for which God has called me heavenward in Christ Jesus." –Philippians 3:13-14 NIV

Day 15 – Read Ephesians 4:31 and write it below. Why is it so essential for us to get rid of the resentment that holds us back?

_____

_____

_____

_____

_____

_____

_____

_____

_____

_____

_____

_____

_____

_____

_____

_____

_____

_____

_____

_____

_____

Praise / Prayer:

_____

_____

_____

_____

_____

_____

_____

_____

_____

_____

Verse for this section: "I do not consider myself yet to have taken hold of it. But one thing I do: Forgetting what is behind and straining toward what is ahead, I press on toward the goal to win the prize for which God has called me heavenward in Christ Jesus." –Philippians 3:13-14 NIV

Day 16 – Remember that resentment typically only affects us and not the person we are holding the resentment against. Have you ever experienced this personally?

_____

_____

_____

_____

_____

_____

_____

_____

_____

_____

_____

_____

_____

_____

_____

_____

_____

_____

_____

_____

Praise / Prayer:

_____

_____

_____

_____

_____

_____

_____

_____

_____

_____

_____

Verse for this section: "I do not consider myself yet to have taken hold of it. But one thing I do: Forgetting what is behind and straining toward what is ahead, I press on toward the goal to win the prize for which God has called me heavenward in Christ Jesus." –Philippians 3:13-14 NIV

Day 17 – Many times our biggest area of unforgiveness can be towards ourselves because of choices or things we have said or done. Have you struggled with forgiving yourself for past mistakes? Explain.

_____

_____

_____

_____

_____

_____

_____

_____

_____

_____

_____

_____

_____

_____

_____

_____

_____

_____

_____

_____

Praise / Prayer:

_____

_____

_____

_____

_____

_____

_____

_____

_____

_____

_____

Verse for this section: "I do not consider myself yet to have taken hold of it. But one thing I do: Forgetting what is behind and straining toward what is ahead, I press on toward the goal to win the prize for which God has called me heavenward in Christ Jesus." –Philippians 3:13-14 NIV

Day 18 – Forgiveness and mercy are the highest items on God's agenda! Forgiveness without mercy can't be accomplished. Do you feel that you are a forgiving, merciful person?

_____

_____

_____

_____

_____

_____

_____

_____

_____

_____

_____

_____

_____

_____

_____

_____

_____

_____

Praise / Prayer:

_____

_____

_____

_____

_____

_____

_____

_____

_____

_____

Verse for this section: "I do not consider myself yet to have taken hold of it. But one thing I do: Forgetting what is behind and straining toward what is ahead, I press on toward the goal to win the prize for which God has called me heavenward in Christ Jesus." –Philippians 3:13-14 NIV

Day 19 – Read Matthew 6:14 and write it below. This is such an important verse for us all! When we forgive others, Christ forgives us. Do you ever feel unworthy of God's love and forgiveness? Why or why not? How does it feel knowing that God will ALWAYS forgive you no matter what?

_____

_____

_____

_____

_____

_____

_____

_____

_____

_____

_____

_____

_____

_____

_____

_____

_____

_____

_____

_____

_____

Praise / Prayer:

_____

_____

_____

_____

_____

_____

_____

_____

_____

Verse for this section: "I do not consider myself yet to have taken hold of it. But one thing I do: Forgetting what is behind and straining toward what is ahead, I press on toward the goal to win the prize for which God has called me heavenward in Christ Jesus." –Philippians 3:13-14 NIV

Day 20 – When we are going through tough times, it's easy to forget about the blessings God has given us. On day 20, write down 20 things that you are grateful for, and spend some time thanking God for all He has done for you.

_____

_____

_____

_____

_____

_____

_____

_____

_____

_____

_____

_____

_____

_____

_____

_____

_____

_____

_____

_____

Praise / Prayer:

_____

_____

_____

_____

_____

_____

_____

_____

Now it's your turn! Write out Philippians 3:13-14 NIV:

_____

_____

_____

_____

_____

_____

_____

Day 21 – There are things in life that we can't control, and sometimes they can be very upsetting. Do you ever struggle feeling that you can't let go of things that are out of your control? Think of a way to remind yourself of letting go of the things you can't control, like a verse on a post-it note, a word to say when you are feeling upset, or a prayer to pray. Write about it and what you hope happens in your life because of it.

_____

_____

_____

_____

_____

_____

_____

_____

_____

_____

_____

_____

_____

_____

_____

_____

Praise / Prayer:

Verse for this section: "Finally, brothers and sisters, whatever is true, whatever is noble, whatever is right, whatever is pure, whatever is lovely, whatever is admirable—if anything is excellent or praiseworthy—think about such things. Whatever you have learned or received or heard from me, or seen in me—put it into practice. And the God of peace will be with you." –Philippians 4:8-9 NIV

Day 22 – As you can see in the stories throughout the book, you are not alone in feeling betrayed, upset, or hurt. How does this give you comfort and hope?

_____

_____

_____

_____

_____

_____

_____

_____

_____

_____

_____

_____

_____

_____

_____

_____

_____

Praise / Prayer:

_____

_____

_____

_____

_____

_____

_____

_____

_____

_____

_____

Verse for this section: "Finally, brothers and sisters, whatever is true, whatever is noble, whatever is right, whatever is pure, whatever is lovely, whatever is admirable—if anything is excellent or praiseworthy—think about such things. Whatever you have learned or received or heard from me, or seen in me—put it into practice. And the God of peace will be with you." –Philippians 4:8-9 NIV

Day 23 – The Bible talks a lot about love and the importance of loving others. Read 1 Corinthians 13:1-13 and write it below. What does this mean to you?

_____

_____

_____

_____

_____

_____

_____

_____

_____

_____

_____

_____

_____

_____

_____

_____

_____

_____

_____

Praise / Prayer:

_____

_____

_____

_____

_____

_____

_____

_____

_____

_____

Verse for this section: "Finally, brothers and sisters, whatever is true, whatever is noble, whatever is right, whatever is pure, whatever is lovely, whatever is admirable—if anything is excellent or praiseworthy—think about such things. Whatever you have learned or received or heard from me, or seen in me—put it into practice. And the God of peace will be with you." –Philippians 4:8-9 NIV

Day 24 – Giving is an essential part of blessing God and God blessing us. It can also re-focus our thoughts, especially when the day is hard. Today, think of a way that you can bless someone–a random act of kindness, a nice note or phone call, helping a friend in need, or volunteering at your church or a local organization… the possibilities are endless. There are so many ways that you can give to others, and I encourage you to make that a part of your life. Write down some ideas and pray over them.

_____

_____

_____

_____

_____

_____

_____

_____

_____

_____

_____

_____

_____

_____

_____

_____

_____

_____

_____

_____

Praise / Prayer:

_____

_____

_____

_____

_____

_____

_____

_____

_____

Verse for this section: "Finally, brothers and sisters, whatever is true, whatever is noble, whatever is right, whatever is pure, whatever is lovely, whatever is admirable—if anything is excellent or praiseworthy—think about such things. Whatever you have learned or received or heard from me, or seen in me—put it into practice. And the God of peace will be with you." –Philippians 4:8-9 NIV

Day 25 – In your final five days to freedom, you will go through five steps to becoming resentment-free.

Step One: Think of your own life. Do you hold any resentment towards anyone? Write about how you have been hurt and the effect it has had on you, your family, or your friends.

_____

_____

_____

_____

_____

_____

_____

_____

_____

_____

_____

_____

_____

_____

_____

_____

_____

_____

_____

_____

_____

Praise / Prayer:

_____

_____

_____

_____

_____

_____

_____

_____

_____

Verse for this section: "Finally, brothers and sisters, whatever is true, whatever is noble, whatever is right, whatever is pure, whatever is lovely, whatever is admirable—if anything is excellent or praiseworthy—think about such things.

Whatever you have learned or received or heard from me, or seen in me—put it into practice. And the God of peace will be with you." –Philippians 4:8-9 NIV

Day 26 – Step Two: Know that God is always there, and it is so important to remember that when times are hard. Romans 8:28 says that God works for the good of those who love Him. Talk about a time where God helped you through a difficult time and how He turned it around for you.

_____

_____

_____

_____

_____

_____

_____

_____

_____

_____

_____

_____

_____

_____

_____

_____

_____

Praise / Prayer:

_____

_____

_____

_____

_____

_____

_____

_____

_____

_____

_____

_____

Verse for this section: "Finally, brothers and sisters, whatever is true, whatever is noble, whatever is right, whatever is pure, whatever is lovely, whatever is admirable—if anything is excellent or praiseworthy—think about such things. Whatever you have learned or received or heard from me, or seen in me—put it into practice. And the God of peace will be with you." –Philippians 4:8-9 NIV

Day 27 – Step Three: Talk to God. Whether it is at church or at home during your prayer time, tell God what is going on. Seek wisdom and insight from Him, and ask for peace as you heal and forgive. Also make sure you continue to talk to someone about your feelings. Don't just hold it in! Write down a plan of action in both of these areas.

_____

_____

_____

_____

_____

_____

_____

_____

_____

_____

_____

_____

_____

_____

Praise / Prayer:

_____

_____

_____

_____

_____

_____

_____

_____

_____

_____

_____

Verse for this section: "Finally, brothers and sisters, whatever is true, whatever is noble, whatever is right, whatever is pure, whatever is lovely, whatever is admirable—if anything is excellent or praiseworthy—think about such things. Whatever you have learned or received or heard from me, or seen in me—put it into practice. And the God of peace will be with you." –Philippians 4:8-9 NIV

Day 28 – Step Four: Hindsight is always 20/20. When analyzing the resentment that you are holding on to, were there things you could have done better? Maybe a better response or using kinder words to the person who hurt you? Today is the perfect time to ask forgiveness from that person. Write down the things you want to say, and then pray over your words. Ask God for direction as you seek forgiveness. This will help you to be FREE from your feelings.

_____

_____

_____

_____

_____

_____

_____

_____

_____

_____

_____

_____

_____

_____

_____

_____

_____

_____

_____

Praise / Prayer:

_____

_____

_____

_____

_____

_____

_____

_____

_____

Verse for this section: "Finally, brothers and sisters, whatever is true, whatever is noble, whatever is right, whatever is pure, whatever is lovely, whatever is admirable—if anything is excellent or praiseworthy—think about such things. Whatever you have learned or received or heard from me, or seen in me—put it into practice. And the God of peace will be with you." –Philippians 4:8-9 NIV

Day 29 – **Step Five:** Remind yourself that you are in control of YOU and not someone else. If there are people in your life that refuse to accept your apology or refuse to apologize for their own actions, forgive them anyway. Write a personal note to yourself, remembering that you can only control *your* part in situations.

_____

_____

_____

_____

_____

_____

_____

_____

_____

_____

_____

_____

_____

_____

_____

_____

_____

_____

Praise / Prayer:

_____

_____

_____

_____

_____

_____

_____

_____

_____

_____

_____

Verse for this section: "Finally, brothers and sisters, whatever is true, whatever is noble, whatever is right, whatever is pure, whatever is lovely, whatever is admirable—if anything is excellent or praiseworthy—think about such things. Whatever you have learned or received or heard from me, or seen in me—put it into practice. And the God of peace will be with you." –Philippians 4:8-9 NIV

Day 30 – Congratulations, you made it through your 30 Days to Freedom! Talk about any changes you have made, and also how you feel. Reflect back on your journal and see how far you've come. Use the remaining pages to write down any thoughts or ideas you might have in maintaining this focus, especially when future situations arise. And take some time to thank God for all He has done in your life. Remember that with God, anything is possible.

_____

_____

_____

_____

_____

_____

_____

_____

_____

_____

_____

_____

_____

_____

_____

_____

_____

_____

_____

_____

Praise / Prayer:

_____

_____

_____

_____

_____

_____

_____

_____

_____

_____

Now it's your turn! Write out Philippians 4:8-9 NIV:

_____

_____

_____

_____

_____

_____

_____

_____

_____

_____

CPSIA information can be obtained at www.ICGtesting.com
Printed in the USA
LVOW04s1624030715

444911LV00007B/85/P